T0197423

DO THE RIGHT THING...

Henry's daughter

WestBow Press
A Division of Thomas Nelson & Zondervan
1663 Liberty Drive
Bloomington, IN 47403
www.westbowpress.com
844-714-3454

Because of the dynamic nature of the Internet, any web addresses or links contained in this book may have changed since publication and may no longer be valid. The views expressed in this work are solely those of the author and do not necessarily reflect the views of the publisher, and the publisher hereby disclaims any responsibility for them.

Any people depicted in stock imagery provided by Getty Images are models, and such images are being used for illustrative purposes only. Certain stock imagery © Getty Images.

Interior Image Credit: Gail Jacalan

ISBN: 978-1-6642-6216-4 (sc)
ISBN: 978-1-6642-6217-1 (e)

Library of Congress Control Number: 2022905849

WestBow Press rev. date: 04/19/2022

WestBow
PRESS®
A DIVISION OF THOMAS NELSON
& ZONDERVAN

It was the last day of school...It had been a long year, and finally it was summer... Little Scotty woke up excited. He hopped out of bed with a big smile on his cute and sweet little face. Scotty is eight years old and lives with his mom, dad and (sometimes annoying) little brother. He was excited, because summer vacation is here at last... He got dressed and hurried downstairs for breakfast. He didn't eat much... He kissed his mom goodbye and ran to wait for the school bus.

His best friend Tim was already at the bus stop. Tim shared that his mom just bought him a new shiny red bicycle for his birthday. Tim was very happy... Scotty and Tim planned to go bicycle riding after school. They planned to ride their bikes together all summer...The last day at school went by fast, and Scotty could hardly wait for the last bell to ring. " RING...RING...RING..."and that was it... school was out!... Hooray!

Scotty ran to get on the school bus with his friend Tim. He hurried home, changed clothes and quickly ate his after school snack. He was so excited, he hardly took a breath...

He told his mom how Tim's mom had bought Tim a new bicycle for his birthday. He asked his mom if it was okay if he went bike riding with Tim. Scotty's mom said "okay, but stay close to home in the neighborhood..." Scotty said "OK...what could happen here anyway?" Scotty went out to the garage and put his helmet on and got on his bicycle. He was so excited. He headed down the driveway towards Tim's. All was going well until all of a sudden he heard yelling... He stopped his bike and looked around... through the trees that line his driveway he could see a commotion across the street. It was the **most horrible thing,** he could hardly believe his eyes...!

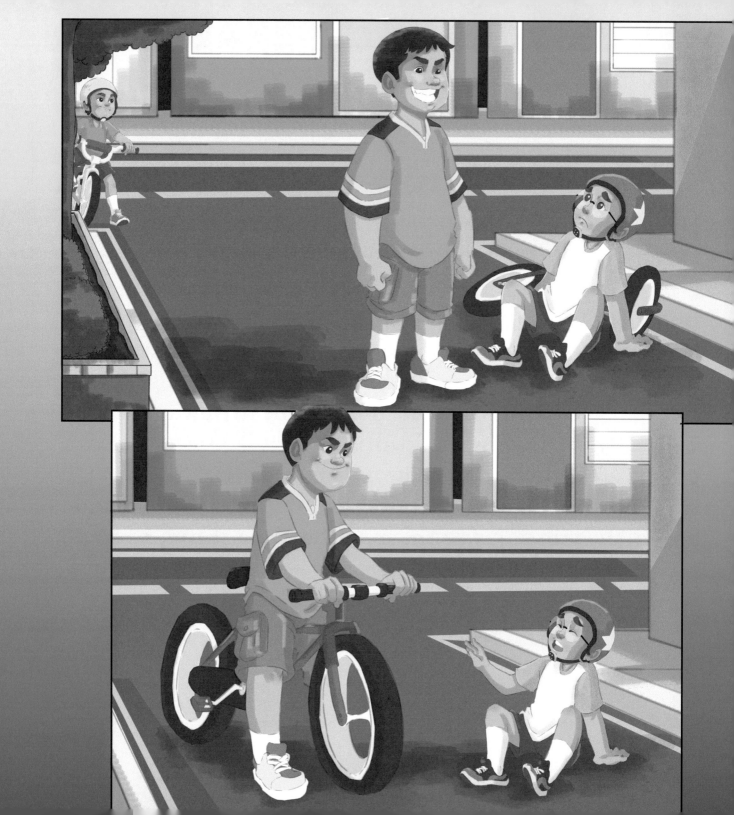

Scotty was in shock...he put his hands up to his face.... and whispered "OH NO"...how could this be happening? He could see his friend was in trouble, very BIG TROUBLE. The local bully had stopped Tim and pushed him off his new bicycle, down on the ground. Then the bully got on Tim's new bicycle and rode off, laughing. Scotty was so scared he felt sick at his stomach, way down deep inside..... he could not move or make a sound...he just sat there for what seemed a long time. Scotty felt he should have gone to help Tim...but he was just too scared. Tim jumped up and ran home crying. Scotty felt sad. He slowly turned around and went back to his garage and put his bike up. He quietly went in the house and into his room. Scotty's mom came in and asked him why he did not go bike riding with his friend. He told her he changed his mind and just wanted to play in his room.

He tried to keep busy in his room for the rest of the evening. He only came out of his room for dinner. Scotty didn't really feel like eating dinner, and just pushed the food around on his plate. He could not wait for dinner to be over. After dinner he quietly took a shower and got ready for bed. After he went to bed, Scotty's dad came in to tell him good night. Scotty was very quiet, and his dad asked if he was okay? Scotty's dad felt something was wrong… Scotty said " I'm OK" and told his dad that he was just tired. That night Scotty did not sleep well at all. He tossed and turned all night…thinking about what happened to his friend. Covers on… and covers off…laying on one side and then the other… he just could not sleep. He felt guilty that he did not try to help his friend… Scotty's friends at school had pointed out the bully (a 6th grader…) and told Scotty to stay away from him or get "beat up".

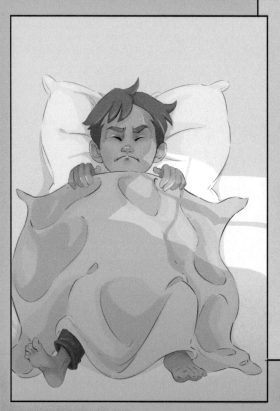

The bully lived on the other side of the school and Scotty hardly ever saw him. Then he remembered what he had heard at church...sometimes NOT speaking up...is just as wrong as telling a lie...That kept running through his mind... Scotty had also learned in Sunday School, that the greatest thing to ever do is love one another...and to follow the "Golden Rule". He knew in his heart he should have helped his friend. To make matters worse, Tim's mom was a single parent and had worked very hard and saved money to buy the bicycle for Tim. To Scotty, it seemed like the night lasted forever... Finally it was morning! Scotty got up and sat on the side of his bed praying.

Scotty's parents are Christians and had taught him to always pray when worried or scared and <u>to do the right thing...</u> even when it was hard. Scotty got dressed and went down to the kitchen. His parents were sitting at the table eating breakfast. With tears streaming down his face, he told his parents what he had seen happen to his friend Tim.

He told them how bad he felt that he let his friend down and how scared he was. Scotty's dad told him that it was okay to be scared… He told him **what really counts is what you do after that**… Scotty told his dad, that in his heart he knew he needed to **do the right thing**… He could have kept quiet and no one would know what he saw. Scotty knew keeping quiet was the wrong thing to do. Scotty's dad gave him a big hug and told him he was very proud of him… and that he did the right thing to speak up. Scotty's mom called Tim's mom and told her what Scotty had seen. Scotty's dad called the police and told them the story.

By the end of the day, the police found Tim's bike at the bully's house and returned the new shiny red bicycle to Tim. Scotty was happy that his friend had his new bicycle back.

Most of all, Scotty was happy that he had learned a lesson… he remembered what he was taught in Sunday School…God and Jesus sees all… and it is always best to do the right thing… even if no one sees it. **Scotty felt good inside now because he finally did "do the right thing…"**

About the Author

Author is a Christian Licensed Marriage, Family and Child Therapist for 35+ years, now retired. She is a mother, grandmother and great grandmother. Each story has a moral value and encourages children to be kind and good to others.

Printed in the United States
by Baker & Taylor Publisher Services